JOURNEYING THROUGH LENT
with MARK

D0730068

Journeying through Lent

with Mark

Daily Meditations

Greg Weyrauch

Augsburg
MINNEAPOLIS

JOURNEYING THROUGH LENT WITH MARK
Daily Meditations

Cover design by Craig Claeys
Book design by Michelle L. Norstad

Library of Congress Cataloging-in-Publication Data
Weyrauch, Greg
   Journeying through Lent with Mark: daily meditations / Greg Weyrauch.
     p. cm.
   ISBN 0-8066-3950-4 (alk. paper)
     1. Bible. N. T. Mark—Meditations 2. Lent—Meditations 3. Devotional calendars. I. Title.

BS2585.4.W49 1999
242'.34—dc21   99-046163

The paper used in this publication meets the minimum requirements of American National Standard for Information Sciences—Permanence of Paper for Printed Library Materials, ANSI Z329.48-1984.   ♾ ™

Manufactured in the U.S.A.   AF 9-3950

03   02   01   00   99   1   2   3   4   5   6   7   8   9   10

CONTENTS

Contents

Contents

A Word to the Reader

Lent is traditionally a time when we Christians take time for a closer look at God and ourselves. Our focus is usually on the life of Jesus and what his life, death, and rising from death mean for us.

This Lenten season—or at any other time of the year—I invite you to journey with me through the Gospel of Mark to find new meaning in Christ for your life and fresh applications of your faith.

The Gospel of Mark was the first written account of Jesus' life. Mark hoped to convince people, as he so passionately believed, that Jesus was the Messiah, the Son of God, the one who would make all creation new. Mark shared the story of Jesus in a straightforward fashion. He gets right to the heart of the story of Jesus, centering on the mission for which God sent his Son—a ministry of preaching, teaching, and healing, a ministry through which God demonstrated unconditional love for each human person and the desire that each of them has a full and whole life.

The preaching, teaching, and healing of Jesus addressed the whole human being. His preaching fed their souls. His teaching nourished their minds. His healing cared for their bodies. As we journey through Mark's Gospel together, let's take some time each day to consider how each of us can become stronger in body, mind, and spirit through our relationship with the God revealed in Jesus Christ.

I encourage you to begin by reading the entire passage from Mark's Gospel for that day and my own reflections on that passage. At the end of each reading you will find some questions to help you ponder the meaning of Mark's words for your life. You may want to keep a journal in which you write down thoughts that come to you. Each reading closes with a prayer.

You may use this book to journey through Mark's Gospel by yourself, but your journey will be even more valuable if you share it with others. At the back of this book you will find a Small Group Study and Discussion Guide.

God bless you as we journey through Lent with Mark. May you be strengthened in body, mind, and spirit to follow Jesus day by day.

Read Mark 1:1-13. *"John the baptizer appeared in the wilderness, proclaiming a baptism of repentance for the forgiveness of sins."*

We begin our journey with Mark—our journey with Jesus, the journey that can transform us and give us new life. We begin where Mark begins, with the good news of Jesus Christ the Son of God. We begin with John the baptizer, the one God sent to prepare the way for Jesus. John fulfilled his calling in word and action by calling people to repentance and by baptizing them with water, for forgiveness and inner cleansing.

To repent means to turn toward God, to recognize that the words God spoke to Jesus at his baptism are addressed to each one of us: "You are my beloved; with you I am well pleased." These words affirm God's promise that he will always be our God, and we will always be his beloved children. As we turn to God, we recognize that all is not as it should be in our lives. There are ways in which our lives are out of harmony with God's song of love.

To repent also means to be transformed. Because God loves us, he wants to change us, to make us more like himself. We are called to live out the meaning of our baptism, day by day, with the old self being drowned and a new self born again daily.

To repent means that we look honestly and fearlessly at ourselves to identify the ways in which we need to grow and change. God gives us light, day by day, to see ourselves more clearly. And by the power of the Holy Spirit with us, God enables us to change, to become more like the Jesus we follow.

What changes are needed in your life so that you can more fully experience God's love for you? How do you need to change in the way you care for your spirit, your mind, and your body?

O God, lead me to see myself clearly, to change what needs to be changed, so that I live in your unending love and share that love with others.

Read Mark 1:14-20. *"And Jesus said to them, 'Follow me and I will make you fish for people.'"*

I remember the day we became the owners of two puppies. The action was taken, against better judgment, because two days earlier we had been forced to put our family dog of thirteen years to sleep. And so we found ourselves looking at dogs from the Humane Society.

We found a litter of pups of unknown ancestry. "The mother is a Doberman, and we think the father is a black Lab," the woman told us. We immediately fell in love with the one male of the litter. It didn't take much persuasion from our children for us to say, "We'll take him."

But then the woman threw us a curve by asking, "How would you like two puppies for the price of one?" We soon became the adopted masters of two pups and, for the most part, we have not regretted it.

We did not choose these puppies because they were obedient. They were not. We did not choose them for their fancy pedigree. We did not choose them for what they could do for us. We chose them because we fell in love with them. And as days went by, these chosen puppies learned to follow us around.

Jesus said to four smelly fishermen, "Follow me." And they dropped everything and followed. Following Jesus, they learned to reach out to others and invite them to follow the Savior, the God of love.

We too have been chosen, not for our obedience or our usefulness to God, but because he loves us with an everlasting love. And drawn by that love, we learn to follow him, day by day, on our journey through life.

Is there anything you need to leave behind in order to follow God more closely? Who is waiting for your invitation to come and follow Christ?

Loving God, thank you for choosing me. Teach me to follow in your ways.

Read Mark 1:21-34. *"And he cured many who were sick with various diseases, and cast out many demons."*

Wherever Jesus went, he changed things. He went to the synagogue to preach and to teach, and people's minds and spirits were changed. He explained the word of God in ways they had never heard. He carried himself in a special way they had never seen. There was a spirit about him that brought the crowds to believe that his words were authoritative and trustworthy.

But Jesus' concern for people went beyond filling their minds with new knowledge and their spirits with fresh religious ideas. He cared about their every need—of mind, spirit, and body. He did not want to burden people with new and more stringent rules for life. He did not come to destroy or even judge them. Instead, he drove out the evil spirits from those possessed. He healed the bodies of those ravaged by fever and disease. He took all in need by the hand and led them to experience a wholeness of body, mind, and spirit that they had never known.

We all have our own weaknesses and problems that keep us from becoming all that God created us to be. Some are physical. Some are mental. Some are spiritual. All can be healed, or at least accepted, so we can be whole before God. Even when we are not immediately cured, we can be healed in ways we often cannot even imagine.

All it takes is to reach out and by faith grab the hand of the Holy One of God. Touched by Jesus, we are healed forever. And we are empowered to reach out with healing for others.

What needs of your body, mind, or spirit can you bring to Jesus today? Are you ready to ask Jesus to touch you in a way that allows you to become all that God wants you to be? Are there any changes you need to make to open the way for God to heal you?

Lord Jesus Christ, please touch my mind, my heart, and my soul that I may make the changes in my life that lead to wholeness within me and around me.

Day 4   Are You Ready to Show Yourself?

Read Mark 1:35–2:12. *"We have never seen anything like this!"*

Some of us can remember when the rite of confirmation included a time when the young confirmands were publicly examined before the congregation with the pastor asking individuals questions about the catechism or Bible. We may not recall what questions we were asked, but we remember vividly the eyes of the congregation on us, the sweaty palms, the dry mouth, the stuttering tongues, the failing memory. No wonder some young people decided after that experience they were done with church forever!

When Jesus told those he healed to go and show themselves to others, he did not send them with a memorized script or a prescribed set of movements. He didn't have to. When someone was touched by Jesus, it showed. The leper's skin was healed of its scars. The paralyzed man could throw aside his mat and walk. Those who observed these healings could not help but say, "We have never seen anything like this!"

When we have experienced the love, forgiveness, and life that is ours through Jesus, we don't need to speak certain required words or act in ways prescribed by others in order for us to show our faith. Those who are loved love naturally. The ones who find true fullness of life in Christ show that they belong to God. We can trust that our way of revealing God's love to others is the right way for us.

Then we can with joy let others see our life in Christ, trusting that it will bring glory to God and attract others to God's way.

What does your care for your body say about your relationship with the Creator? What does the way you tend to your mental life say about your relationship with the one who said we should love God with all our minds? What does your care of your spirit show about your relationship with the Holy Spirit?

O God, may your love, life, and forgiveness show in every word I speak, in every thought I think, in every action I take, and in every relationship you offer me.

Read Mark 2:13-17. *"When Jesus heard this, he said to them, 'Those ho are well have no need of a physician, but those who are sick; I have come to call not the righteous but sinners.'"*

I hate to hear people say, "I won't come to church because it's full of hypocrites." They're right, of course. If we ran all the hypocrites out of the church, the buildings would be empty. At times we all are hypocrites. We say one thing and do another. We fail to live up to the life demonstrated by Jesus. But that's not the whole story.

I love the bumper sticker that says: "Christians aren't perfect—only forgiven." By coming to our world in the person of Jesus, God has revealed that he accepts and loves us in our imperfections, that he forgives us for all the hypocritical things we do and say, and that he promises us to make us new—in this life and more perfectly in the life to come. Jesus said that he came for those who know they need help.

For that reason, I shy away from those who seem to be so certain of their faith and their ideas of what other Christians and the church should be and do. I squirm when I speak with someone who blames God or the devil or their parents or their spouse for all the problems in their life, but I enjoy counseling with those who admit their mistakes and ask, "What can I do to get straight with God and with other people?" I love it when someone says, "I am not perfect." Jesus came for people like that. He came for all of us. And he wants us to reach out to others with all the love that is in us.

Thanks be to God, who wants to be with sinners like you and me, and who has taken the initiative in Jesus Christ to make us forgiven people, new people, whole people.

What group of "sinners" do you tend to avoid? Is there a group of people outside the church that you could reach out to with the gifts, resources, and experiences God has given you?

Forgiving and loving God, I thank you that you continue to love me even when I sin, even when I am a hypocrite, even when I fall far short of the life revealed in Jesus. Lord, use me as your forgiven child to bring your love and forgiveness to others.

Read Mark 2:18-22. *"And no one puts new wine into old wineskins; otherwise, the wine will burst the skins and the wine is lost, and so are the skins; but one puts new wine into fresh wineskins."*

Tradition can be paralyzing. It can keep us from change, from stretching ourselves and opening ourselves to new approaches to faith and life. It can close the door on God's Holy Spirit. By rejecting new ministry opportunities and new ways of doing old ministries, tradition can give the impression that God's Spirit moved only in the past, that God is no longer alive and active in our world today.

There are many new wineskins waiting to be filled today. Though in some places the number of church members are declining, the number of people seeking to grow spiritually is increasing at a rapid pace. We who have continued to worship, to share our God-given talents in the ministries of Christ's church and to carry on its traditions also need to be open to change in ourselves and in the church. In this way the old forms can be filled with the new life available to us in a relationship with God through Jesus Christ.

We can actively search for new ways to carry out the ministries of preaching and teaching and healing to nurture bodies, minds, and spirits. It will take change, but Jesus was God's agent of change, sent so that you and I and all God's children might find wholeness and salvation forever.

How open are you to changes in the way our church carries out its ministries? What changes are needed for the "new wine" of God's Spirit to be poured out in your congregation? How can you change so that you are more open to God's Spirit?

Lord, set us free to be open to the kinds of change in our lives and our church that will allow your Spirit to flow freely among us and through us.

Read Mark 2:22–3:6. *"Then he said to them, 'The sabbath was made for humankind, and not humankind for the sabbath; so the Son of Man is lord even of the sabbath.'"*

The secularization of our society has resulted in the loss of one of God's greatest gifts: the Sabbath, a weekly day of rest.

When God had accomplished the creation, he spent the seventh day at rest. He then shared the gift with us, saying, "Remember the Sabbath day to keep it holy." To be holy means for something to be what God created it to be.

The Sabbath is God's gift to us to keep us healthy in body, mind, and spirit. It reminds us that we do not have to earn God's favor by working seven days a week. He offers us a day of re-creation, which is needed more than ever in our fast-paced lives as a time to rest our bodies, nourish our minds, and renew our spirits.

It is also a day when we gather to worship with other believers. Worship provides us the opportunity to renew our relationship with God and others. In word and sacrament we experience God's grace. It's a gift we need each week. It is healing for our spirits. It is a time that, used wisely, can renew our minds and make us ready to follow Jesus in the week ahead. He is the Lord of the Sabbath, and he offers the Sabbath to us as his gift of love.

How well are you doing at taking one day a week as a Sabbath? How do you use that time? What are your favorite ways to find refreshment for your body, your mind, and your spirit?

Lord of all time, move us to use your time wisely, caring for all you have given us—body, mind, and spirit. We thank you especially for the Sabbath, your gift to us. Help us to accept that gift and use it well.

Read Mark 3:7-19. *"He went up the mountain and called to him those whom he wanted, and they came to him."*

One of the joys of watching puppies is seeing how rapidly they grow and learn. One of their first learnings is to respond to their names when someone calls them.

The first time my wife and I tried to walk our new puppies on a leash, the male took to it immediately. The female, named Angel, was another story. She sat down and resisted every coax, every tug, every pull. I began to think our puppy was sorely misnamed.

Finally my wife walked to the corner with the male puppy and began to call, "Come, Angel." The puppy stood up slowly. Suddenly she sprang forward, jerking my shoulder from the socket, and began to race toward my wife at a speed exceeding the ability of my arthritic knees to keep pace. Angel responded to a loving call, and since then it has been a pleasure to take her for her daily walk.

Most of us were chosen by God in our baptism. There God calls us each by name. He tells us that he loves us forever. He tells us he will walk with us forever. He gives us the gift of the Holy Spirit, and that Spirit within us will make us become all that God intends for us. Listening to that call of God, we learn to follow him, day by day, and to walk in his ways.

How do you hear the call of God in your life? Are there any ways in which you are resisting God's call to move forward? What is one thing you need to do today to respond to God's call?

Lord God, we thank you that you have called us in baptism and that you continue to call us day by day. Enable us by the power of your Spirit to hear your call and to follow you.

Read Mark 3:20-30. *"Truly I tell you, people will be forgiven for their sins and whatever blasphemies they utter."*

The promise of Jesus is clear: people will be forgiven for their sins—all their sins. That forgiveness is freely offered. The only thing that can keep it from us is if we resist the Holy Spirit by refusing to accept Jesus' promise of forgiveness.

Sometimes we put human limits on God's forgiveness. We don't forgive as God does, and so we try to limit God's ability to forgive too. We look at terrible situations in the world or we think about those who have sinned against us, and we say, "I can forgive anything but that!"

When we are tempted to limit God's forgiveness in that way, we need to return to Jesus and remember that he has conquered the powers of the evil one. He is ready to cleanse us from the evil spirit of resentment and revenge. He has promised to forgive us all sins, even our lack of forgiveness. And by remembering that promise, we are set free to forgive all those near us or far away.

Is this a foolish idea? Jesus' own family members thought he was out of his mind. And the religious leaders accused him of being on the side of evil. But the promise of Jesus still stands: God wants to forgive all the sins of all humanity. And he wants us to share that forgiveness.

Are there any ways in which you have trouble accepting God's forgiveness for yourself? Are there ways in which you limit God's forgiveness to others? Who is waiting for you to speak a word of love and forgiveness today?

Your promise of forgiveness is true, O Lord. Open our ears to hear it. Open our hearts to feel it. Open our arms to share it.

Read Mark 3:31-35. *"Whoever does the will of God is my brother and sister and mother."*

Jesus was surrounded by a crowd, probably people eager to hear him, to receive his help and healing. Then his mother and his brothers showed up, and it sounds as if they were looking for preferential treatment. They send in a message: "We're here."

We might expect Jesus to ask the crowd to make room for his family so they can take a special place near him. But Jesus often surprises us. His thoughts are not always ours. In this case Jesus says, "Look around you. All these people—all who do the will of God— are my brothers and sisters and parents."

By his action and his words Jesus expands our idea of family. The good news is that as Christians we are members of Christ's family—a worldwide family that crosses all barriers of age, gender, race, nationality, and economic level. We may not have a human family, or our human family may not be what we wish it were, but in the church we can find ourselves as part of God's family. We are no longer alone. In the family—in the community—we can become all we were meant to be.

And, while God expects us to love and care for our human family, he opens our eyes to see a much larger family. He gives us a love that is big enough for all the world, for the whole creation, for all humanity.

Everywhere we look we see our mother and father, our sisters and brothers, joined in love to do the will of our heavenly Father.

Where have you most experienced being part of God's family? In what ways are you reaching out to those beyond your immediate family?

Thank you, heavenly Father, for making us part of your worldwide family. Help us to do your will by reaching out in love to all our brothers and sisters.

Read Mark 4:1-20. *"And these are the ones sown on the good soil: they hear the word and accept it and bear fruit, thirty and sixty and a hundredfold."*

What kind of soil are you?

Are you like the path, so hard and tough that God's word never gets through?

Are you like the rocky soil? Was there a time when you felt you heard God's word for the first time? Did it fill you with joy? Did you hunger and thirst for every opportunity to hear God's word and to be with God's people? But did the feeling fade? Did worries or troubles turn your attention elsewhere?

Or are you like the soil filled with thorns? Are you so busy with job, house, family, entertainment, and other commitments that your relationship with Christ occupies second place at best—that you set aside no time for God's word and for prayer?

Or are you like the good soil—hearing God's word, doing your best to give it the proper place in your life, treasuring it and sharing it with others in word and action?

If we see ourselves honestly, with the insights God gives, we probably recognize that we are all four kinds of soil at different times—sometimes impervious to the word, distracted by worries or troubles, overwhelmed by other priorities, and at times—thank God—grateful hearers and doers of the word.

What does Jesus see when he looks at you? What kind of soil would you be in his eyes? What does your life say to others about where your priorities lie? How can you open yourself more fully to hear God's word?

In word and sacrament you come to us, O Lord, with the nutrients of your Holy Spirit, to strengthen us and help us grow. Open us to hear your word and do it, day by day.

Read Mark 4:21-25. *"Pay attention to what you hear; the measure you give will be the measure you get, and still more will be given to you."*

Sometimes I, as a pastor, get discouraged about my seeming inability to get others to hear the word of God. I'm frustrated when I see the empty pews, when confirmation students seem totally uninterested, when councils and committees are reluctant to implement new programs. I feel like I have put my lamp on a lampstand for others to see, and yet it seems I make no difference.

At times like this I try to remind myself of Jesus' promise, "Pay attention to what you hear; the measure you give will be the measure you get, and still more will be given to you." It's his way of promising that his word will bring blessings—results will follow our efforts to let our lamps shine.

All of us are called to shine like lamps in a dark world. All are given the word of God to share in our families, our neighborhoods, our world. At times, we may become discouraged at the seeming lack of results. That is the time to remember that our job is to speak God's word and to do acts of kindness. We are not responsible for the results. Those who hear our words or see our light are responsible for their own responses. We can act and speak with confidence, trusting that God will give the blessing.

⁓

How can you in your daily life share a word from God? How does your congregation live out its mission to bring that word to all those who have not yet heard it?

O God, may your light shine through us, through the words of love and life we speak to others.

Read Mark 4:26-29. *"The earth produces of itself, first the stalk, then the head, then the full grain in the head."*

I remember when our grandson Nathan, then sixteen months old, did something for the first time that really tickled out hearts. Each night as we sit at the dinner table, we fold our hands and bow our heads for a table grace. Ever since Nathan has sat in a high chair and joined us for dinner, we had been teaching him to fold his hands and bow his head with us. Because he was usually served before the rest of us, we would have to stop him from eating first. One evening, to our surprise and joy, we found him patiently waiting for us all with folded hands and a great big grin.

All by itself the earth produces grain, Jesus says. That word that is sown in our hearts will take root and produce a good crop. The example we set will make a difference in the lives around us. Our attempts to teach our children and grandchildren loving ways will bear fruit.

At times we may doubt whether that word is having any effect in our lives. It may look as if our attempts to teach our children God's ways are not taking hold. It may seem as if our struggles to make a difference for God in our workplace or community just aren't doing any good.

That's the time to return to the one who gave us the word, who sends us into mission, who promises us, "The earth produces of itself, first the stalk, then the head, then the full grain in the head."

What evidence do you see around you of God's word bearing fruit? In what ways are you trying to make a difference for God in your home, workplace, and community? In which situations do you most need to trust Jesus' promise that the earth will produce a good crop?

Lord, when we are discouraged about our attempts to pass on the faith or make a difference in the world, help us to hear your promise and trust the power in the seed.

Read Mark 4:30-34. *"It is like the mustard seed, which, when sown upon the ground, is the smallest of all the seeds on earth; yet when it is sown it grows up and becomes the greatest of all shrubs, and puts forth large branches, so that the birds of the air can make nests in its shade."*

When the good news is proclaimed, when that word is incarnated in the church, when the love and mission of Jesus Christ is shared within a community of believers, there will inevitably be growth. Jesus tells us it isn't optional. It's the natural outcome.

Many people rejoice in this growth, glad that new people are finding sustenance and shelter in the church. But there can be resistance to growth too, because growth inevitably means change. Some church members may feel that the congregation is no longer a comfortable family in which everyone knows everyone else. Some may say, "Why can't we stop growing? I miss things the way they were." Out of frustration, some may even choose to leave the congregation.

We need to remember that Jesus never dreamed small dreams. His hope is that one day all humanity will know and experience God's love. His hope is that each one of us will grow, and that together, as a congregation, we will grow not just in numbers but in faith, in understanding, in love, in the longing to bring others into the home of the church.

———

What barriers to change do you experience that keep you or your congregation from growing spiritually? How can those barriers be removed so that growth can freely take place?

O God, you are the Father of all humanity and the creator of all that exists. Stretch our faith and trust in you that we may branch out and become all you hope for us to be.

Read Mark 4:35-41. *"He said to them, 'Why are you afraid? Have you still no faith?'"*

Fear is one of the strongest motivators for human behavior. Fear can paralyze us, causing us to avoid certain people, places, and situations. Fear can move us to do and say things that harm other people. Fear of God, in a negative sense of being afraid of God, can keep us from fully experiencing his love and forgiveness.

Fear of God, in the positive sense of awe or respect, is what the disciples experienced when Jesus calmed the storm. It's a fear that says, "Yes, there is a God, a God of power and love, and I belong to that God!"

Believing in such a God can be frightening, because it asks us to surrender any pretense that we have control over God's creation, over our own lives, over other people. But the truth is that God is in control, not us. We have life only because God has given it. We love only because God loves us. We have forgiveness only because God acted to forgive us through the life, death, and resurrection of Jesus Christ our Lord.

But believing in such a God also takes away our fear. Nothing depends on us. It all depends on God—salvation in this life and in the life beyond. We belong wholly to God, and God has the love and the power to keep us safe—for all eternity.

———◦———

What fears keep you from loving God with all your heart, soul, and mind? What fears keep you from loving others as you love yourself? What fears keep our church from becoming all God calls us to become? How can those fears be overcome?

Lord, in this story of the calming of the storm we see your power and your love. Help us to yield ourselves to you. Take away the fears that keep us from loving you, ourselves, and others as you love us.

Read Mark 5:1-20. *"Go home to your friends, and tell them how much the Lord has done for you, and what mercy he has shown you."*

The demon-possessed man who came to Jesus for help could not be bound by chains on his hands and feet. No one was strong enough to subdue him. Only Jesus could drive out the demons that possessed him. Once the demons were gone, the man was bound to Jesus forever. He was bound to share the story of how Jesus' touch has made him new forever. He felt so bound to Jesus that he wanted to leave his family and all that he possessed to follow Jesus. He was bound by Christ to become a living testimony of God's mercy.

With the waters of Baptism and the word of God, each of us has been bound to Christ too. He cleanses us, too, from the demonic, destructive forces within us. He has promised his healing touch on us—body, mind, and spirit.

Believing in these baptismal promises leads us to acknowledge our identity as children of God. It inspires us to love as God loves. It fills us with the confidence that nothing can ever separate us from God. It binds us to God with a strength that can't be overcome by anything. It sends us into God's world with a living message of hope and joy. Whatever good we do, we do because God has bound us to himself forever.

What destructive forces keep you from experiencing God's touch? What demonic powers can you help to drive out from this world? What binding thoughts and practices in our congregation do we need to break in order to carry God's message of hope and love to the world?

Lord Jesus, you bind us to you forever through Baptism and your promises. Break all the chains, real and imagined, that bind us. Set us free to free others in your name.

Read Mark 5:21-43. *"Immediately aware that power had gone forth from him, Jesus turned about in the crowd and said, 'Who touched me?'"*

Individuals thirst for power—in their jobs, in the community, in their homes, even in their churches. Often that thirst for power is revealed in what people buy, the clothes they wear, the cars they drive, the neighborhoods in which they live. This thirst for power over others can destroy families, companies, communities, churches, and even God's creation.

There is only one power that can bring us true fullness of life. There is only one power that can heal broken relationships and damaged lives. There is only one power that lasts forever. This is the power that God offers all humanity through Jesus Christ.

Jesus used his power to heal people's bodies, minds, and spirits as he healed this woman who reached out to him in the crowd. Now he makes his healing power available to us. Reach out to Jesus today in faith, and he will fill you with the power of God's love and forgiveness, a power that will make you one with God and God's creation, a power that will give you strength to endure whatever you encounter in this life and forever. Reach out and open yourself to the healing power of God for your body, your mind, and your spirit.

What physical, mental, or spiritual weaknesses would you like Jesus to strengthen? Ask Jesus to show you the way to strength, health, and wholeness.

Lord Jesus Christ, you have the only power that can bring true healing. Lead us to open ourselves to your power for our every need of body, mind, and spirit.

Read Mark 6:1-6a: *"They said, 'Where did this man get all this? What is this wisdom that has been given to him? What deeds of power are being done by his hands!'"*

Have you ever thought that if you had lived when Jesus was on earth and seen him do his miracles and heard him teach that it would be easier for you to have faith? That seems plausible, but the record we have in the Bible shows us something else.

The friends of Jesus and his family in Nazareth knew him only as the son of Mary and Joseph, brought up to be a carpenter like his father. He was one of them, part of the working class. They found it very hard—nearly impossible—to believe that this young man was the promised Messiah, the Son of God.

Their lack of faith in him must have been hard for Jesus too. We're told that he was "amazed at their unbelief."

Martin Luther was right when he said, "I cannot by my own reason and strength believe." Believing in Jesus goes beyond logic and human understanding. It moves from the mind into our hearts. And such living faith is always a gift of God's spirit. We can't manufacture it in ourselves, but we can ask God to strengthen our faith and make it more real.

It's one thing to know about Jesus and another to know him, to have a relationship of love and faith with him. We all need to know about Jesus—what he did, what he said. But he wants more than that. He desires a relationship of love and life with each of us that lasts forever.

<hr />

Do you know facts and stories and teachings about Jesus, or do you know him as you know a friend? How might you open yourself more fully to experiencing friendship with Jesus?

Lord Jesus Christ, you lead us to believe. Help us to move beyond a faith of the mind to a faith of the heart that says yes to you and to your vision for our lives.

Read Mark 6:6b-13. *"He ordered them to take nothing for their journey except a staff; no bread, no bag, no money in their belts."*

Jesus called his twelve disciples and sent them out two by two to do the kind of work that Jesus himself did: to teach and heal. It must have been scary for them—to be doing something new, taking nothing for the journey, depending on the generosity of others. But they went—and did wondrous things in Jesus' name.

Twice I have been called to develop a new congregation for our denomination. Thank God my instructions were not as challenging as those Jesus gave his first disciples! Still it was risky to leave an established congregation for the uncertainty of a new ministry. Hitting the streets and ringing doorbells and inviting individuals to become part of a church that has not even begun to meet for worship is a challenge! But I thank God that he has introduced me to people and places I would not have chosen had he not led me. Both new ministries have been challenging, and both have been rewarding beyond my dreams.

God has ways of calling each of us to new ways of service in our congregations, our communities, our world. This may involve risks and uncertainties with what seems like inadequate resources of talents or time or money. Believing can be challenging, but believing that Jesus walks with us when God calls us to new paths can result in experiences that help us grow in our relationship with God and with other people.

How have you resisted God's nudge to go as God's servant? Into what new ministries is God nudging your congregation? How can you make these part of the ministry of Christ?

Lord, lead us to see the new opportunities for ministry to which you call us. Enable us to move forward with confidence to meet and accept whatever challenges as your followers and as your church.

Day 20   Believing Can Be Perplexing

Read Mark 6:14-20. *"When [Herod] heard [John the Baptizer], he was greatly perplexed; and yet he liked to listen to him."*

King Herod was perplexed about John the Baptizer. This fearless preacher in the desert had the audacity to criticize Herod for taking his brother's wife, Herodias. To silence John, Herod put him in prison. But when Herodias wanted to kill John, Herod protected him, fearing that he might indeed be a righteous man. John's words perplexed Herod, but he continued to listen to John. Eventually, though, he gave into pressure from Herodias and had John killed.

Later Herod was also perplexed about Jesus. He didn't know what to make of Jesus. Some were saying Jesus was Elijah or one of the other Old Testament prophets. Others were saying that Jesus was John the Baptizer risen from the dead—and that idea really threw fear into Herod.

Believing can be perplexing. We are confronted with many alternative ideas in newspapers, magazines, radio, TV, and classrooms. Events in our own lives may raise doubts about God and his love for us. We may often wonder what to believe.

Doubt is a natural part of faith, part of the process of spiritual growth. The God who is faithful to us accepts us with our doubts. We bring our doubts to him, discuss them with our pastor and with our brothers and sisters in the church. We can continue to listen to God and his word and trust that the Spirit will lead us all to truth.

What perplexes you most about the Christian faith? What perplexes you about your relationship with God? What resources do you have for dealing with your questions and doubts?

Lord, when I am perplexed about questions of faith and life, remind me to bring those doubts to you. Help me to continue to listen to you, as you speak to me through your word and through the words of my fellow believers.

Read Mark 6:21-29: *"Immediately the king sent a soldier of the guard with orders to bring John's head."*

Someone has said, "The trouble with Christians nowadays is that nobody wants to kill them anymore." That is not true, of course. In many parts of the world—in Africa, the Near East, and Asia—Christians are being persecuted and even killed for their faith.

It's true that in the United States we don't have to worry about a politician chopping our head off because of our faith. We don't have to worry about bullets or bombs or mines from members of another religion. Yet believing in Jesus can still be dangerous.

We know how dangerous it can be among friends, relatives, or coworkers to break the rule that says, "Never discuss religion or politics." Do you speak of your faith outside the doors of your church? Does your neighbor know that you are a Christian? Do your coworkers? Do you speak of your relationship with God with your own family? We know they will not kill us, but fear of embarrassment or rejection keeps us silent when we could speak out and share our faith with someone who needs it.

But there is a more subtle danger. Believing is dangerous if we keep it to ourselves, because that keeps us from growing. It keeps us from knowing others as fellow children of God and from sharing God's gift of Jesus.

God can give us the kind of courage that John the Baptizer had—to speak God's truth even when it is risky or unpopular. It may be that we will suffer in some way for it, but it will be worth it—for our own sakes and for those who hear us.

What perceived dangers keep you from sharing your faith with others? What can you do to overcome these fears and reach out to those who need to hear about God's love and care and forgiveness?

Lord, lead us to quit playing it safe as your witnesses and to move forward in faith together that all humanity might know you and your love.

DAY 22   JESUS IS A MASTER CHEF

Read Mark 6:30-44: *"Taking the five loaves and the two fish, he looked up to heaven, and blessed and broke the loaves, and gave them to his disciples to set before the people; and he divided the two fish among them all."*

My mother was a master chef in a working-class family with seven children. The main dish of many meals filled our stomachs not only once, but twice. We all know that Sunday's ham or roast or chicken would return later in the week in a soup or casserole, and that it would usually be more tasty the second time around. Mom had a way of taking leftovers and using them to make a meal fit for a king.

Jesus was surrounded by five thousand hungry people. Presented with only five loaves of bread and two fish, he was able to satisfy their hunger—and fill twelve baskets with leftovers. And I thought my mother was a miracle worker!

In our Sunday worship, you and I may come to the Lord's table with a spiritual hunger that we think no one can possibly satisfy. We may doubt whether a crumb of bread and a sip of wine will even begin to satisfy our needs. Yet, in the word that is spoken and in the sacrament received, we receive a feast for our souls. We experience the presence of the living Lord, his forgiveness, his love, a hope for all the days that lie ahead of us. Jesus, the Master Chef, has prepared a meal for us that fully satisfies our hearts and minds. And it's only a foretaste of the feast to come!

Which hunger of your soul do you most want Christ to satisfy today? What is someone around you hungering for that you can give them? What hungers in our community are crying out for nourishment from our church?

Lord Jesus, you are a miracle worker. You feed our bodies, minds, and spirits with all we need. Lead us to share that bounty with the hungry we encounter today and every tomorrow.

Read Mark 6:45-46. *"Immediately he spoke to them and said, 'Take heart, it is I; do not be afraid.'"*

One sunny summer afternoon in Wisconsin, when our children were small, we were sitting on the back patio of the home of my wife's parents on the shores of Lake Michigan. With the water as smooth as glass, we decided to take the children for a Sunday-afternoon ride in the family boat. We launched the boat in the public harbor and began to head north toward Racine. It was a perfect day for boating on the lake, even for our small seventeen-footer.

Suddenly the winds shifted from south to northeast. The clear skies grew dark and ominous. We huddled together in the cold. I reversed course and headed back to harbor, as fast as the fifteen-foot waves would allow. After a half-hour trip that seemed like a day, we returned safely to the harbor. Just as I jumped from the boat to the dock, the heavens broke loose with a cold, driving rain. I backed the trailer into the raging waters, grabbed both children from my wife's arms, and we rushed to the car. I paused to say, "Thanks, God, for keeping us safe!" As we turned the corner toward home, the storm ceased as quickly as it had begun, and a rainbow arched across the sky.

We've all encountered days when life is going well; the weather of our spirit is sunny. Then storms strike without warning—illness, death, problems at home or on the job. Then Jesus speaks to us, as he spoke to the disciples in the boat, "Take heart, it is I; do not be afraid."

The storms may not cease immediately, but eventually they do subside, and we are reassured of God's loving care. There is no storm that the Master Meteorologist cannot still!

How did God bring you through a stormy time in your life? What people have been rainbows in your life, signs of God's promised love in the midst of life's storms? How can you be a rainbow for someone else in a stormy time?

Lord, thank you for the ways you have brought us through the storms of life. Help us to share your love with those we find in stormy times today.

Read Mark 7:1-23. *"You have a fine way of rejecting the commandment of God in order to keep your tradition."*

The religious leaders came to Jesus and criticized his disciples for not following all the rules that were part of the Jewish tradition. In his response to them we see Jesus as the Master Communicator, challenging, critiquing, pointing people beyond human rules to the deeper truths of God.

Jesus did not mince words. He communicated his thoughts, his feelings, and his faith honestly. He spoke simply, explaining God's ways in earthly terms so people could understand him. He spoke out strongly to those whose words and actions were not consistent with God's plan for all humanity—that we should love God with all our hearts, minds, and souls, and love our neighbors as ourselves. Yet he never sought to harm anyone with his words. He sought not to condemn but to heal.

Jesus is still the Master Communicator. He continues to communicate with us through his written and spoken word, through the words we speak to one another. As Jesus' followers, we can learn from him to be master communicators of God's truths. We can learn to focus on God's truths rather than on human traditions. If we find it necessary to confront someone, we can do it not to condemn but to heal. We can keep it simple like one of the great theologians who, when he was asked to summarize the Christian faith, replied, "Jesus loves me. This I know, for the Bible tells me so."

Are there ways in which you see human rules or traditions getting in the way of God's truths? What could you do to better communicate the love of God to those around you? How could our church better communicate God's truths to those who have yet to hear it and respond?

Lord, your word is truth. Lead us to speak it more clearly that all humanity may hear your good news and live it.

Read Mark 7:24-30. *"But she answered him, 'Sir, even the dogs under the table eat the children's crumbs.'"*

When this woman came to Jesus, seeking healing for her daughter, he first said no to her plea. It seemed as if Jesus was rejecting her, as one of the "dogs," the unacceptable outsiders, but she continued to look to Jesus for help. She did not give up.

"No" is not one of our favorite words. Few of us will reach out again once we have been rebuffed or rejected. In my ministry, I've encountered many men, women, and children whose first response to my invitation to become a member of the church has been "No." I remember Bob, who had been "burned" by his experience in another congregation and said, "Never again." But he went on to become president of our congregation and gave a generous gift that guaranteed the groundbreaking of our church building. I remember Phil, whose first response was "We haven't gone to church for years." Yet after continuing invitations he responded by calling me and saying, "We want to join your church." And his family went on to become tithers of their time and talent and treasures. Some have disappointed me and some have surprised me, and I thank God that he has encouraged me never to give up on any of them.

That's the message of Jesus, the Master Motivator. He came for all people—even those considered outsiders, the "dogs" who can hope for no more than crumbs from his table. He motivates us to reach out, to love, to feed, to heal, and to never give up.

———

What person or group who once rejected you needs a second chance? How can we better reach those outsiders who have felt rejected by the church or who are rejecting the church?

Lord, motivate us to reach out to those who seem to be outsiders. Give us patience and love to keep on reaching out.

Read Mark 7:31-37. *"They were astounded beyond measure, saying, 'He has done everything well; he even makes the deaf to hear and the mute to speak.'"*

Time after time in Mark's Gospel we encounter healings performed by Jesus that show his concern not only for the minds and spirits of people, but also for their physical needs.

My grandmother was deaf by the time I was born. She had lost her hearing and her husband almost simultaneously in her late forties. During most of my childhood she lived with my family. My relationship with her meant much to my physical, mental, and spiritual development.

Grandma was eating right long before modern nutritionists. She read voraciously—novels and biographies. She wrote poetry and was a regular contributor to the "Letters to the Editor" column of our local paper. She demonstrated to me in word and action what it meant to be a Christian, by worshiping weekly, singing the liturgy in an enthusiastic monotone, and most of all loving me and encouraging me to become all that might be possible with the gifts God had given me. And she did it all with deaf ears!

Her deafness only opened her life to new possibilities for experiencing life in this world. She was surely touched by the hand of Jesus and found healing in him that increased her desire to live for God in this world.

Reflect on how one who was handicapped affected you and your life. What was opened to you because of this relationship? How can you and your church reach out to those with physical needs?

Lord, none of us is perfect. In our imperfections we thank you for your total acceptance, and we ask that we might reach out and touch whose who feel less than whole with that same love and healing power you offer through Jesus Christ our Lord.

Read Mark 8:1-21. *"And he sighed deeply in his spirit and said, 'Why does this generation ask for a sign?'"*

Stop signs. Danger signs. Speed limit signs. If we ignore them, we can get into big trouble.

The Pharisees and even Jesus' disciples share a human flaw with us modern creatures: a failure to see and to respond to the signs around us.

Every hungry stomach fed, every hurting hand healed, every parable preached by Jesus was a sign of who he was and what God was trying to accomplish through him. Yet the religious elite, the inner circle of the twelve, and almost everyone missed the signs that were there before their eyes, the signs revealing Jesus' identity and God's purposes through him.

It obviously tried and tired Jesus. It probably still tries and tires him today when he hears our grumbling and he asks the same questions of us: "Why are you talking of having no bread? Do you still not see and understand? Are your hearts hardened? Do you have eyes to see and ears to hear and still not understand?"

Jesus not only gave us signs about himself and God's will for humanity, but he was the Master Sign. If anyone wants to know who God is, they need only look to Jesus. When we see Jesus healing, teaching, feeding, suffering, and dying for us, we can know of God's care for us. And then when we see the sign of Jesus rising from death, we can be sure of God's power to give us new life.

How are Jesus and his words and actions a sign for you of God's identity? How can you be a sign of God's love for others?

Lord, help us to recognize the signs of your love and power we see revealed in Jesus. Help us to lift high his cross, the sign of your salvation and love.

Read Mark 8:22-30. *"He asked them, 'But who do you say that I am?' Peter answered him, 'You are the Messiah.'"*

The Apostle Paul defined his relationship with Christ in terms of servanthood. He saw himself as a slave, with Christ as his master. Paul contended that once Jesus Christ has taken hold of your life, you had no choice other than to serve him and all humanity.

Peter's answer to Jesus' question "Who do you say that I am?" is much the same. With his answer he means "You are the Messiah, the Christ, the one promised to the Hebrews for centuries, the one who would make all things new, the one who would save all humanity from sin and death forever. You are the Son of God. You are the Master of all Masters, the only one worthy of our servanthood."

The difference between Christ and anyone or anything else that might enslave us is that Christ's chains set us free. They have freed us from all our fears. Death no longer has a lock on us. Sin no longer needs to bind us. We are free from the need to be our own god. We are free to serve the one who loved us so much he was willing to die for us, and who rose to show his power over death. We are free to serve the Master of all Masters.

What chains keep you from really knowing and following Christ? What chains keep our church from really being the "body of Christ" in the world? How can we find Christ's freedom from all that binds us?

Christ Jesus, you came to set us free from the chains that enslave us. Help us to follow you freely as loving slaves of the Master of all Masters.

Read Mark 8:31–9:1. *"For those who want to save their life will lose it, and those who lose their life for my sake, and for the sake of the gospel, will save it."*

You could call this one of the "hard sayings" of Jesus. It is a troubling paradox—those who want to save their lives will lose them, but those who lose their lives on behalf of Jesus and the gospel will actually save them. What are we to make of this? Is it an invitation to martyrdom? Well, certainly, both in history and in the world we live in, many Christians have suffered physical persecution and death for their faith, and we believe their lives are saved in God.

Our belief in eternal life, however, does not exhaust the meaning of this text. So many of us try to "save" our lives by storing up the things of this world—wealth, possessions, power, prestige. Rather than save our lives, however, we lose them to the very things we thought would give us security. We become slaves to our money, our possessions, and the opinions of others, and, rather than enjoy our lives, we find ourselves obsessed, worried, and fearful. Jesus promises that those who give up trying to save their lives with the things of this world will find abundant life in the things of God— love, mercy, peace, justice.

How does this hard saying of Jesus sound in your ears? What choices could you make that will lead you into abundant life with God?

Lord, we struggle with your words that call us to lose our lives for your sake. Please show us how we may receive the new life that comes only from you.

Read Mark 9:2-13. *"Then a cloud overshadowed them, and from the cloud there came a voice, 'This is my Son, the Beloved; listen to him.'"*

The greatest need each of us has is for love. We need to know it in our minds. We need to experience it in our hearts and share it with others.

Put yourself in the place of Peter, James, and John that day on the mountain of transfiguration. Can you imagine what they experienced? How did they feel when they saw Jesus glorified in front of them? How did they feel when they saw the two great men of old, Moses and Elijah, with Jesus? How did they feel when they heard the words "This is my Son the Beloved"? Surely they experienced the love and presence of God in a whole new way.

We may never have such an unusual mountaintop experience as those disciples. Yet we experience the love of God in simpler, less dramatic ways. When we witness a baptism in church, we are reminded that God has placed his seal of love on each of us. Each time we receive Holy Communion, we taste that love of God in the bread and wine. In the church we experience the love of God through fellow believers, through their friendship and care.

The message of all this is clear: we belong to God. God loves each of us as his beloved child. As we experience that love, we reach out and share it with others around us.

Where do you most experience God's love for you? Who needs your love and God's love today? How can you help them taste that love?

Lord, I want to taste your love. I want to love you in return and love my neighbors near and far.

Read Mark 9:14-32. *"Jesus said to him, 'If you are able!—All things can be done for the one who believes.'"*

It was a Sunday morning several years ago. I was in the midst of a serious crisis in our family. I didn't know what I was going to do. I was physically drained, mentally exhausted, spiritually empty. I felt like a failure as a father, a pastor, a man. I hadn't slept at all, but spent the night crying uncontrollably.

And now I had to lead two worship services, preach, teach an adult class, baptize a child. There was no other pastor on the staff I could call on to fill in for me. How could I possibly do what I had to do that morning? I felt all alone.

I left for church earlier than usual. Standing in the sanctuary I stared at the cross on the back wall. At first no words would come. Finally I whispered, "Lord, I don't know how I can do it today. If anything is going to happen here this morning, you will have to do it. I'll stand here, but the words will have to be yours.

I don't really know how it happened that morning. I remember that a layman saw the pain on my face and offered to pray for me. I know that two worship services happened. Two sermons were preached. A child was baptized.

I do know that "All things can be done for the one who believes." The Lord proved it to me that day.

———⌒⌒⌒———

Has there been an experience in your life when God helped you do what you felt was impossible? Is there something you now consider impossible that you can look for help from God?

Lord, you alone can make the impossible possible. Expand our vision of what can be possible with you by our side.

Read Mark 9:33-50. *"Have salt in yourselves, and be at peace with one another."*

When his disciples argued about which of them was the greatest, Jesus settled the matter quickly. The greatest would be the servant, the one who would welcome a child in his name, the one who would give a cup of water in Jesus' name, the one who would be like salt to season and preserve this world.

The Sunday after my grandson Nathan was born, these words were read in church: "Have salt in yourselves, and be at peace with one another." As I held Nathan in my arms, I nicknamed him "Salty."

A couple of years later, it was the first Sunday in December, the traditional day for our congregation's annual meeting, the day in which we consider the budget for the year to follow. Annual meetings are not one of my favorite aspects of ministry. Too often they fail to bring out the best in people. And so on the days that lead up to the meeting, I'm often on edge. My family and coworkers know enough to stay out of my way.

This year, however, something happened that made things go better. At the close of the second service, as I stood at the rear of the church during the singing of the last hymn, my grandson ran to me with arms outstretched. I lifted him up, and he gave me a hug filled with love and peace. "Salty" and I greeted the departing worshipers together, and all the anxiety and tension drained from me.

I went on to have the most positive annual meeting I've ever experienced!

———————

Who has seasoned your life with peace? Thank them today. Who needs a salty taste of peace from you today? Go and spice up their lives. What situations in our community are waiting for God's salt and peace from our congregation?

Lord, shake us like salt from the shaker, so we can be at peace with each other and be peacemakers in our families, our places of work, our community, our world.

Read Mark 10:1-16. *"Let the little children come to me; do not stop them; for it us to such as these that the kingdom of God belongs."*

Few of us dream of becoming a child again. We don't want to go back to the past, to being dependent for everything we need, to being under the control of others, to the bullies and name-calling of elementary school, to the struggles and fears of adolescence, to the search for a vocation, to the struggles of the first years of adulthood. We're glad that childhood is behind us.

But Jesus says that childhood is also a part of our present and future. In fact, he says the hard words: "Whoever does not receive the kingdom of God as a little child will never enter it." Being a child before God means giving up our pretensions of being in control, having all the answers, knowing just what to do in each situation. God invites us to let go and be a child before him.

We can be a child in our physical being, acknowledging that all we have and are is a gift of the Father of all creation. We can thank him for those gifts in words and actions that reflect our responsibility to the giver of these gifts.

We can be childlike in our mental being, realizing that we don't have all the answers, recognizing that we have not yet tapped the potential of the brain God has given us. We can experience the joys of being lifelong learners about God, his ways, and his world.

We can be childlike in our spiritual being, rejoicing in being his children, leaving room in our lives for the mystery and presence of God.

We can taste the truth that, as God's beloved children, we belong to the kingdom.

What gift of childhood have you left behind that could bring greater joy and zest to your life today? What can you do to be more like a child in your relationship with God?

Father God, you are the source of our being and we are your beloved children. Restore to us the joys and the freedom and the growth of childhood.

Read Mark 10:17-31. *"But many who are first will be last, and the last will be first."*

The rich man came to Jesus and asked, "What must I do to inherit eternal life?" Jesus said, "You must sell all you have and give it to the poor." The disciples were amazed. If that's what it takes to inherit eternal life, then who can be saved? Jesus told them, "For mortals it is impossible, but not for God; for God all things are possible." It is God who makes the first last, and the last first. It is God who gives us eternal life.

In response to God's initiative, we take a new look at the question, "What must I do?" God calls us to give to the poor, to share the wealth he has given us. God calls us to distribute the wealth of his creation, the physical gifts of the world, that all humanity might be physically well. God calls us to distribute the wealth of his wisdom, that each human mind might be opened to the wonders of knowledge and reach its God-given potential. God calls us to distribute the wealth of his love, that all humans may experience emotional well-being and care.

The one who invites us to taste eternity, also invites us to follow him each day of our lives.

The rich man's wealth kept him from following Jesus. Is there anything in your life keeping you from following the one who offers you eternal life?

———◦———

What kind of wealth has God given you and your congregation? How could you be sharing that wealth with others?

Lord, you call us and give us a taste of eternal life. Remove from our lives the barriers and burdens that keep us from following you. Help us to see new ways of sharing the wealth you have given us.

Read Mark 10:32-45. *"But whoever wishes to be first among you must be your servant, and whoever wishes to be first among you must be slave of all."*

One of the reasons I continue to be a Green Bay Packers fan lies in the greatness of their late coach, Vince Lombardi. One of Lombardi's players, the Hall of Fame defensive tackle Henry Jordan, was asked by a reporter what it was like to play football for such a demanding coach. Jordan responded, "Ah, shucks, it's easy. There are no favorites. He treats us all the same—like slaves!" Though they may have felt like slaves, most of the Packers of that successful era also loved Lombardi like a father.

Jesus tells us that the greatness of each one us lies in our ability to be a servant—a servant of God, a servant of those around us. The greatness of Jesus was shown no more vividly than when we took a bowl of water and a towel and washed the feet of his friends (see John 13). As they were served by Jesus, they tasted his greatness, and they learned from his example and followed it.

Taste greatness. Get on your knees in humble service to the Lord and then get up and go to those who need your love and help today.

Think of someone who has shown you their greatness by serving you. Let them know how you feel about them today.

———◦———

In what ways are you being a servant of God in the world? Are there any new ways you can taste the greatness of being a servant of Jesus?

Lord Jesus, you showed us that the possibility for true greatness lies within each one of us. Help us to find joy in being your servants and the servants of those who need us.

Read Mark 10:46–11:19. *"Jesus said to him, 'Go; your faith has made you well.' Immediately he regained his sight and followed him on the way."*

Jesus responded to blind Bartimaeus' cries for help with a question: "What do you want me to do for you?" When Bartimaeus responded, "Let me see again," Jesus healed him.

Jesus didn't wait for others to come to him. He hit the streets and went to the people. He met them where they were and then asked what he could do to help them. Then he healed their bodies, minds, or spirits. Or he fed them or met their other needs.

Jesus gives us a great example for responding to others in need. Too often, as individuals and as a church, we look before we leap. In a misguided effort to save the world, we devise new ministries without taking time to involve ourselves in meaningful conversation with those we hope to help. Such efforts may lead only to frustration for them and for us.

Instead we can begin by the simple act of listening. We can get to know those to whom we are reaching out—know their real hurts and problems. If we're not sure how we can help, we can ask. Then we will be ready, like Jesus, to respond with help that is really needed.

Let's hit the streets and find the hurting and ask what we can do to help.

Have there been times when you held back from helping because you didn't know what to do? What are some ways our church could go to the people of our community and learn their needs?

Lord, open our ears, our minds, our hearts, our arms, so that we might bring your healing love to those in need with the healing they really need.

Read Mark 11:20–12:17. *"So I tell you, whatever you ask for in prayer, believe that you have received it, and it will be yours."*

When Jesus' opponents tried to trick him by their questions, he answered with questions of his own. As we see in this passage, his questions and his answers challenged both his opponents and his followers. They are all flustered by the challenge to define John's ministry of baptism, they are angered by the implications of the parable of the Wicked Tenants, and they are "utterly amazed" by his solution to the dilemma of paying taxes.

To move their hearts and minds and spirits, Jesus knew he had to encourage them to find answers for themselves. He never discouraged them from asking questions, even if he was sometimes frustrated by their lack of understanding.

This freedom to ask questions, to explore the life of faith is the same freedom God gave Adam and Eve in the Garden. It's the same freedom God gave the Israelites wandering in the wilderness. It's the same freedom God gave David and all the other kings. It's the same freedom God gave Isaiah and the other prophets as they tried to share the messages God gave them. It's the same freedom God gave Paul and the missionaries of the early church. It's the same freedom he gives you and me today to seek answers to the questions of life in prayer, in word and sacraments, in the fellowship of the church.

Because God has set us free to seek, we can ask our true questions and ask for what we really need from God, trusting in God's promise that if we ask in faith, we will receive.

What questions of faith would you like God to answer for you? Who or what might help you find the answer?

God, keep putting questions in my mind that lead me to know you better, serve you more lovingly, and share you more boldly in all I do and say.

Read Mark 12:18-34. *"You shall love the Lord your God with all your heart, and with all your soul, and with all your mind, and with all your strength. . . . You shall love your neighbor as yourself."*

Jesus cut through all the myriad commands given to Moses at Sinai and all the interpretations by later Hebrew scribes and priests and left us with two brief sentences to guide us in our relationships with God and our neighbors: Love God. Love your neighbor as yourself.

Watching what Jesus commands leads us to watch what Jesus loved. He loved God. We see his intimate relationship with the Father in his prayers and in his actions, demonstrating that he and the Father are one. What Jesus said we can understand as the word of God. What Jesus did we can understand as the will of God.

Jesus also loved his neighbors. Time after time he gave totally of himself so that the bodies, minds, and spirits of others might be whole. Jesus was love personified. He didn't love only the lovable; he loved all humanity. And he was willing to give his life that all others might live in the grace of God.

Guided by Jesus' commands, following his example, set free by his salvation, we are led to a life of love—love for God and love for our neighbor.

⌇

What does it mean for you to love God? What are the ways in which you express love for your neighbor?

Lord Jesus, in the pages of your word we see your love for your Father and your love for those you encountered in your life on earth, your love expressed on the cross. May your love kindle in us love for God and those around us.

Read Mark 12:35-40. *"Beware of the scribes, who like to walk around in long robes, and to be greeted with respect in the marketplaces, and to have the best seats in the synagogues and places of honor at banquets!"*

Again we see Jesus in conflict with his opponents, the scribes, the experts in the Jewish laws. Part of their problem was that they focused on laws, on the minute regulation of daily conduct, rather than on the love and grace and mystery of God. And, though they may have been careful to obey certain religious rules, they were guilty of religious arrogance and hypocrisy.

Jesus was different. In all his teachings we see the message of grace shining through: God loves you. God forgives you. God answers your prayers. And Jesus' life demonstrated the message, as he went about doing good in humble service.

God calls us all to be bearers of his message wherever we are— at home, at church, at work, in our communities—to bring the good news of Jesus Christ. And God calls us to bring healing to bodies and minds and spirits of those we meet. We are called to share the good news in words and to live the good news in deeds of kindness.

In our religious life today do you see examples of spiritual leaders who emphasize law rather than gospel? How can we bring the good news to people who have been taught to think of religion as a matter of keeping rules?

Lord Jesus, thank you for your warnings against teachers who are not worthy of our trust. Help us to teach the good news of your love and to live out that good news in our daily lives.

Read Mark 12:41-44. *"He sat down opposite the treasury and watched the crowds putting money into the treasury."*

Jesus was an observer of human behavior. He watched what they did and said. He saw whether their actions matched their words. He had an unusual insight into people that allowed him to determine if they were all they claimed to be. He could see beyond outer appearance into a person's mind and heart.

In the story we read today we see him sitting in the temple watching as people brought their tithes and offerings to the temple treasury. He saw rich people throwing in large amounts. But it is a poor widow who really caught his eye with her gift of two small copper coins. Her gift so touched him that he called his disciples together and commended her as an example for them to follow. He looked at her and saw that she have given all she had for God and God's work.

What does Jesus see when he observes people bringing their offerings to our church? Does he see people giving comfortably out of their abundance? Does he see some giving sacrificially, like the widow? What does our giving say about our character, our faith, our gratitude to God?

We know that Jesus' way of judging our giving is not based on the dollar amount. It is based on the attitude of our hearts, the priorities of our lives. He looks at us with eyes that see truth and with eyes filled with love.

What is the attitude of your heart when you give? How do you think Jesus would evaluate the way you spend your money?

Lord, lead us to give our all for you and for your people.

Read Mark 13:1-31. *"Heaven and earth will pass away, but my words will not pass away."*

The thirteenth chapter of the Gospel of Mark is filled with Jesus' description of the end times of this world and the culmination of the kingdom of God. It is not a pretty picture. Jesus describes the distress of the times as unequaled from the beginning of time. He says that relationships will change, and his followers will need to stand firm in their relationship with him. He refused to give the exact time these things would happen and warns his disciples to beware of those who make those kinds of predictions. Jesus describes a time when the very order of creation will be shaken, but God's faithful will be saved and God's word will never pass away!

Jesus' words in this chapter do not answer all our questions about what will happen or when. But they do proclaim with certainty that these things will happen—in God's own time. Nothing anyone can do will change his mind, his schedule, his plan for the fulfillment of his kingdom. It all depends on God.

What we can do is to watch and wait, trusting in God's word. There is comfort in knowing that the same God who created the universe, the same God who loved us so much that he sent his Son to die for us, the same God who raised his Son from death will be the one in charge when this world passes away and his kingdom is fulfilled.

Do you anticipate the coming of God's kingdom with fear or with joy? Why? What words of Jesus in this chapter give you hope? How might these words influence the way you care for your body, your mind, and your spirit?

Lord, help us to look with hope to the coming of your kingdom in all its completeness and to trust in your word of promise.

Read Mark 13:32-37. *"And what I say to you I say to all: Keep awake!"*

Jesus warned his disciples a second time against predicting the time of the end of the world. There will always be false prophets who offer their detailed blueprints and schedules for the end of time. And they will always find a hearing, because people are frightened by insecurity. They long for the comfort of knowing exactly what is going to happen. But such predictions always offer a false security, Jesus says.

Jesus tells us another way to live. He warns us against getting too comfortable against spiritual drowsiness. His words are meant to stab us awake: "Don't let God find you spiritually asleep. Be alert! Keep awake!"

It's easy to be lulled into spiritual sleep. We can be lulled by entertainment, by distractions, by alcohol and drugs—even by an overloaded schedule. All these things can dull our bodies, our minds, and our spirits. We need time and space to be awake to the spiritual realities of our life, time to be alert to our priorities, time to be alert to God's word and God's presence in our lives.

Are there ways in which you are tempted to spiritual slumber? What changes would you have to make in your life to respond to Jesus' call: "Keep awake!"

Lord, we confess that we can easily get overly comfortable and lazy in our spiritual lives. Help us to hear your wake-up call and to make the kind of changes that keep us spiritually alert.

Read Mark 14:1-31. *"Then he took a cup and after giving thanks he gave it to them, and all of them drank from it. He said to them, 'This is my blood of the covenant, which is poured out for many.'"*

What captures your mind and heart when you receive the sacrament of Holy Communion? Is your focus on your own need for God, for forgiveness, hope, healing, meaning for life? Do you find yourself reflecting on Jesus, on the greatness of his gift for all humanity—his life for ours, his obedience for our disobedience, his blood for our sins? Do you think of the community gathered to share that special spiritual meal with you, others who share your sin and your forgiveness, your life and your relationship with Jesus our brother?

Holy Communion is a rich feast indeed. It encompasses all these meanings. Jesus Christ, the brother of us all, is there as our host. We experience his presence in the bread and wine. We experience the presence of our brothers and sisters in faith. We come and find forgiveness, new strength, and new love—gifts of Jesus our brother.

What does it mean for you to think of Jesus as your brother? What does Holy Communion mean to you?

Lord Jesus, you are our brother in life and death and for eternity. We thank you for the gift of your body and blood in Holy Communion. May they strengthen our bond with you and with all our sisters and brothers.

Read Mark 14:32-72. *"Keep awake and pray that you may not come into the time of trial; the spirit indeed is willing, but the flesh is weak."*

In this passage, we see several cases where the spirit was willing, but the flesh was weak. The disciples can't help but fall asleep in the garden; a young man was following Jesus, but then fled; and, of course, Peter denies knowing Jesus. We can see ourselves so many times in this chain of events. We understand from our own experiences the ineptitude of the disciples, the frightened escape by the young man, and the outright denial of our Lord.

In our spirits, we know that we should stay awake, stay near, and stand up for Jesus. But we fail. Jesus knows we will fail him. He even predicted it to Peter. But he understands us. He knows that our spirits are willing and our flesh is weak, and he loves us and calls us in spite of it. We can find comfort in that.

When have you wanted to stand up for what you believe in, but found yourself falling down instead? How does this story of the disciples' actions challenge or comfort you?

When I am unable to stay awake for you, Lord, forgive me. Help me to find the strength I need to do your will.

Read Mark 15:1-41. *"At three o'clock Jesus cried out with a loud voice . . . 'My God, my God, why have you forsaken me?'"*

It was three o'clock in the morning. I felt totally alone as I stood in the sanctuary of our church. It was dark in that room, in my mind, in my heart, in my soul. The only light was from one small lamp that shined over the hand-carved scene of the Last Supper at the front of the altar.

Twelve hours earlier my father had died, unexpectedly, suddenly, as his heart exploded within his chest. I was suffering. I was angry. I was hurt. My body shook with chills and uncontrollable sobs. My heart pounded in an irregular rhythm. My spirit was empty. And here I stood on this dark place, where in sixty hours I would have to preach a Christmas sermon. I felt forsaken, hopeless.

And then God came to me as God has come to so many others. In a still small voice, he spoke to my very soul: "If you believe what you preach, you need not grieve for your father without hope. The one whose birth you soon celebrate has defeated even death. Your dad is in good hands. And my Son, in time, will heal you too."

A peace, coming from Jesus our brother in suffering, then filled my body, mind, and spirit, and I began the slow sure process of recovery.

Where have you found healing and hope when you were suffering? What can you do to bring healing and hope to someone who is suffering? What suffering in the world can your church meet with healing and hope?

Jesus, our brother in suffering, your healing and hope are forever. Send us to our brothers and sisters in suffering, that we might bring healing to them as you bring healing to us.

Read Mark 15:42-47. *"Then Joseph bought a linen cloth, and taking down the body, wrapped it in the linen cloth, and laid it in a tomb that had been hewn out of the rock."*

From the moment we leave our mother's womb, there is a common destination we all share. Death happens to us all. In spite of the miracles of modern medicine, death is inevitable. Death is a part of life.

Jesus, the Son of God, shared our entire human existence. To live as we live, he had to die as we die.

Joseph of Arimathea, a follower of Jesus, in a great act of courage, went to Pilate and asked for permission to bury the body of Jesus. He then lovingly wrapped Jesus' body in a cloth and placed it in a tomb hewn out of rock. And to protect the body, he sealed the entrance to the tomb with a large stone.

Joseph thought that was the end of it—but it wasn't!

Jesus is our brother in death, but that's not the end of it for him—or for us!

———

What is your greatest fear concerning death? How do the life and teaching of Jesus answer those fears?

Jesus, you are our brother in life and in death. You saved yourself from nothing that you might save us from everything.

Read Mark 16:1-8. *"Do not be alarmed; you are looking for Jesus of Nazareth, who was crucified. He has been raised; he is not here."*

Jesus is more than our blood brother, more than our brother in suffering, more than our soul brother. Through his resurrection from death, he became our brother forever!

Where I live, the opening day of baseball season is an exciting event, signaling the end of a long winter, providing the opportunity to see old friends again, and to laugh and shout and share new dreams for the success of the hometown team. There's excitement in the air!

That is nothing like the excitement of that first Easter, as the women heard the amazing news that Jesus the crucified was no longer in the tomb. He was alive, and they would soon see him again. No wonder they were filled with terror and amazement.

The resurrection signaled the victory of Jesus over sin and death. Now the way was open for all humanity to experience new life, new hope, new power. Now the way is open for us to experience true wholeness—of body, mind, and spirit. Now the way is open to bring all humanity together in joy and celebration. Now the way is open for us to be with Jesus our brother, forever!

In what parts of your life, or in the life of the church, do you see a need for new life, a new beginning, a resurrection? How does Jesus' resurrection give you hope for this new life?

Thank you, God, for the miracle of Jesus' resurrection and the miracles he makes possible in our lives today and every tomorrow.

SMALL GROUP STUDY AND DISCUSSION GUIDE

This study and discussion guide for small groups is designed for seven weekly meetings during the Lent-Easter season, or at any time of year. It assumes that the participants will read the daily meditations and reflect on the meaning for their lives. In the small group there will be time for further study of the Gospel of Mark and sharing of personal insights.

WEEK ONE

Read Mark 1:1–3:6. Discuss the following questions.

1. What made John the Baptizer such a striking messenger? What was the heart of his message? How did people respond?
2. What do you learn about Jesus from his baptism and temptation?
3. Who were the first disciples Jesus called? How did they respond to his invitation? What new task did he give them?
4. What two things did Jesus do in the synagogue at Capernaum? What impressed people about Jesus' teaching?
5. What do Jesus' acts of healing reveal about him?
6. What do you learn about the prayer life of Jesus from Mark 2:35? How might you follow his example?
7. After his work of healing and concern for others, what need did Jesus evidently have? How did he handle this? What does this suggest for your life?
8. What did the friends of the paralyzed man do for him? What is the first thing Jesus did for the man? Why is that significant?
9. The religious teachers criticized Jesus for his actions. What do Jesus' answers to them tell you about him and the kind of people he wants as his followers?
10. What pictures did Jesus use to contrast the religious life he offers with that of the Jewish religion of his time? Are there "old wineskins" in your life? Explain.
11. What situation gave Jesus' opponents another chance to put him on the spot? Explain Jesus' question in Mark 3:4. When have religious rules gotten in the way of your care for people?

Look back at the reflection questions in the meditations for Days 1-7. Choose the ones you would most like to discuss in your group.

SMALL GROUP STUDY AND DISCUSSION GUIDE

WEEK SIX

Read Mark 10:46–13:37. Discuss the following questions.

1. How did Bartimaeus show the depth and persistence of his faith in Jesus? How did Jesus respond to his faith?

2. Imagine Jesus coming to you today and asking, "What do you want me to do for you?" How would you answer him?

3. When Jesus entered Jerusalem, how did the crowd respond to him? How did their reaction fall short of true discipleship?

4. On the way into Jerusalem, why did Jesus curse the fig tree? Why did he act as he did in the temple?

5. In Mark 11:24, what great promise did Jesus make? According to Mark 22-25, what conditions must be met in order for our prayers to be answered?

6. In Jesus' parable in Mark 12:1-12, what does each of these represent: vineyard, owner, tenants, servants, heir? Who are the others to whom the vineyard will be given?

7. How did Jesus' opponents try to trap him with questions about taxes and life after death? How did he foil their attempts?

8. In Mark 12:28-34, what does Jesus identify as the two great commandments? How are you living out those commandments day by day?

9. In Mark 12:35-44, what was Jesus' criticism of the religious leaders? What meaning can we take from this?

10. What signs did Jesus give that would precede the destruction of the temple? To what extent are these signs being fulfilled also in our time? What promises does Jesus give in Mark 13:1-13?

11. What encouragement is there in Mark 13:31? What does it mean for your life?

12. To what event does Jesus compare the suddenness of his return? In view of that, what is your attitude or stance?

Look back at the reflection questions in the mediations for Days 36-42. Choose those you would most like to discuss in your group.

Small Group Study and Discussion Guide

Week Seven

Read Mark 14:1–16:8. Discuss the following questions.

1. Why did some people criticize the action of the woman at the home of Simon? List all the reasons Jesus gave in her defense. What might we learn from her example?

2. In Mark 14:12-26, why do you think Jesus instituted the Lord's Supper at this time?

3. On the way to the Mount of Olives (Mark 14:26), what bad news did Jesus give his disciples? What good news?

4. What attitude toward God his Father did Jesus exemplify in his prayer?

5. Think back over the recent chapters. What evidence is there that Jesus was going to his death knowingly and willingly?

6. What did Jesus reveal about himself in his trial before the Jewish religious leaders?

7. Why do you think Peter denied Jesus? How might he have avoided doing that?

8. What was the charge the religious leaders apparently brought against Jesus, as revealed by Pilate's question? What was the irony of this charge?

9. What was the stated reason for the crucifixion of Jesus? What was the real reason?

10. In your present understanding, what is the significance and meaning of Jesus' death?

11. What was the significance of Jesus' words, "My God, my God, why have you forsaken me?"

12. How did the women react to the news that Jesus is risen? How do you respond?

Look back at the reflection questions for Days 43-47. Choose those you would like to discuss with your group.

Small Group Study and Discussion Guide

Week Two

Read Mark 3:7–4:34. Discuss the following questions.

1. What witness did the evil spirits give to the identity of Jesus? Why do you think Jesus silenced them?

2. In Mark 3:13 we again see Jesus withdrawing from the crowds. What was his purpose this time? What tasks did he give his apostles?

3. How did Jesus' family react to his popularity? Why do you think they responded this way?

4. How did the teachers of the law explain Jesus' power? How did Jesus uncover the flaw in this explanation?

5. How would you explain what is meant by the sin against the Holy Spirit? Why can it not be forgiven?

6. When they arrived on the scene, what did Jesus' mother and his brothers do? According to Jesus' explanation in verse 35, are you a member of his family?

7. Using Jesus' explanation of the parable of the sower, explain in your own words what he meant by each of the kinds of soil. What kind of ground are you? What changes in your attitude or lifestyle would make you more receptive to the good seed of God's word?

8. What point is Jesus making in the analogy of the lamp?

9. How does Mark 4:26-29 help you understand how God's kingdom progresses on the earth?

10. What does the parable of the mustard seed illustrate about the kind of growth God can cause?

Look back at the reflection questions in the meditations for Days 8-14. Choose which ones you would most like to discuss in your group.

WEEK THREE

Read Mark 4:35–6:29. Discuss the following questions.

1. What seems to have been the disciples' attitude toward Jesus sleeping in a storm? Have you ever felt that Jesus was "asleep" during a crisis in your life? Explain.

2. How did Jesus criticize his disciples? Does this criticism apply to you?

3. Describe the man who came to Jesus in the region of the Gerasenes. What did the man who had been demon-possessed ask Jesus (Mark 5:18)? How does Jesus' reply help you understand why God sometimes does not give us what we ask for?

4. Why is Jairus an unlikely person to come to Jesus for help? How did he show his faith in Jesus?

5. What was the attitude of those who brought Jairus the news of his daughter's death? How is Jesus' attitude different?

6. What did Jesus encounter in his "hometown" of Nazareth (Mark 6:1-13)? How did the local people respond to him? How did they limit what Jesus could do for them?

7. How did the twelve apostles carry on Jesus' work? In what ways are you actively involved in teaching and healing or in promoting such work done by others?

8. As news of Jesus spread, what were some common opinions people had of him? Who did Herod think Jesus was?

9. Why had Herod arrested John the Baptizer? Why did Herod kill John?

10. Can you recall a time when you did something wrong in order to please others? What could help you resist these pressures in the future?

Look back at the reflection questions in the meditations for Days 15-21. Choose those you would like to discuss in your group.

SMALL GROUP STUDY AND DISCUSSION GUIDE

WEEK FOUR

Read Mark 6:30–8:30. Discuss the following questions.

1. How did Jesus meet the needs of people in Mark 6:30-44? What part had the disciples played in meeting these needs?

2. How did the disciples react when they saw Jesus walking on the water? How did he respond to them?

3. Why did Jesus refer to the Pharisees and teachers of the law as hypocrites? What really was the problem with their kind of religion?

4. How did some of the people in Jesus' time use religious tradition to set aside the commands of God (Mark 7:9-13)? Can you think of any parallels in your life?

5. In Mark 7:24-30, who was the woman who confronted Jesus and what did she want? How did she respond to Jesus' seemingly sharp comments? What qualities in Jesus must she have recognized and appealed to?

6. Describe the way Jesus healed the man in Mark 7:31-37. Why do you think he proceeded in this way?

7. Compare the event in Mark 8:1-13 with the feeding of the five thousand in Mark 6:30-44. Which details are the same? Different?

8. Why do you think the Pharisees were so blind to Jesus' true identity?

9. In Mark 8:14-21, what was Jesus saying about the Pharisees and Herod by his use of the word "yeast"? How did the disciples misunderstand Jesus' message?

10. Describe the way Jesus healed the blind man at Bethsaida. If this incident is viewed as having symbolic meaning, what do you think Mark is suggesting about the disciples' spiritual vision?

11. How did Peter show that his spiritual eyesight was improving?

Look back at the reflection questions in the meditations for Days 22-28. Choose those you would like to discuss in your group.

WEEK FIVE

Read Mark 8:31–10:45. Discuss the following questions.

1. How did Jesus explain what kind of Messiah he would be? Why did Peter deserve such a sharp rebuke from Jesus?

2. What specifically does it mean for you right now to take up your cross and follow Jesus?

3. In Mark 9:1-13 what promise did Jesus make to his disciples? How was Jesus' promise fulfilled six days later?

4. While Jesus and the three disciples were on the mountain, what problem were the other disciples facing? Why did Jesus seem to be so exasperated? What did the father's response reveal about him?

5. How did the disciples show that they still misunderstood Jesus and his kingdom (Mark 9:33-41)?

6. What is the secret of being first in God's eyes? Why would a child be a good model for Christ's teachings about this attitude?

7. What is salt like? How can Christians be like salt in the world?

8. According to Jesus in Mark 10:1-16, why did Moses allow divorce? How did Jesus underscore God's ideal of the permanence of marriage?

9. How would you answer the question in Mark 10:17? How did Jesus answer the question? Why do you think the man responded as he did?

10. In Mark 10:32-45, what journey did Jesus and his disciples begin? What did Jesus say would happen there?

11. How is the life of Jesus' followers to be different from that of Gentiles (nonbelievers)?

12. What is the ultimate form of service that Jesus will render? How do you think this gift of life will be a ransom?

Look back at the reflection questions in the meditations for Days 29-35. Choose those questions you would like to discuss in your group.